Popular French Cookery

By Mary Berry

Dolphin Press

Photographs on pages 14, 15, 19, 22, 23, 27, 38, 47, 51, 55, 59, 91 by courtesy of Syndication International
Photographs on pages 11, 30, 31, 42, 63, 67, 75, 79, 83, 86, 87 by courtesy of Paf International

First published by Octopus Books Ltd

This edition published by Treasure Press
59 Grosvenor Street
London W1

© 1972 Octopus Books Ltd

ISBN 0 907407 46 3

Printed in Hong Kong

This edition produced for:
Dolphin Press, 9150 S.W. 87th Ave.,
Suite 108, Miami, Florida, U.S.A.

Contents

Weights and Measures   8

Curtain raisers: Beginnings   9

Top of the Bill of Fare 33

Supporting roles: Vegetables and Salads. 58

Intermission: Cakes and Pastries 72

Last Act: Desserts 81

Index 92

WEIGHTS AND MEASURES

All measurements in this book are based on Imperial weights and measures, with American equivalents given in parenthesis.

Measurements in *weight* in the Imperial and American system are the same.
Measurements in *volume* are different, and the following table shows the equivalents:

Spoon measurements

Imperial	U.S.
1 teaspoon (5 ml.)	$1\frac{1}{4}$ teaspoons
1 tablespoon (20 ml.)	$1\frac{1}{4}$ tablespoons (abbrev: T)

Level spoon measurements are used in all the recipes

Liquid measurements

1 Imperial pint	20 fluid ounces
1 American pint	16 fluid ounces
1 American cup	8 fluid ounces

CURTAIN RAISERS: BEGINNINGS

In France, these are known generally as *hors d'oeuvres*, but this term, outside France, has a specific meaning. Better, I think, to call the first course beginnings, for this is what it is – the beginning of a meal which should leave both you and your guests mellow and satisfied. The course should have two virtues – first, it should titillate the palate but not destroy the appetite, and, second, it should be easy to prepare and to serve, so that you, as cook, may concentrate on the main course without worry. Most of the recipes that follow may be prepared beforehand.

Stuffed Peppers
Poivrons farcis

4 large green peppers

Filling:
1 small aubergine (egg plant)
3 tablespoons ($3\frac{3}{4}$T) olive oil
1 large onion, chopped
1 oz. (4T) flour

12 oz. cooked ham, cubed
pepper
$\frac{1}{2}$ teaspoon dried oregano
$\frac{1}{2}$ pint ($1\frac{1}{4}$ cups) chicken stock
2 tablespoons ($2\frac{1}{2}$T) tomato
    purée
salt

Cut the peppers in half lengthways, remove the seeds and stem. Cut the aubergine (egg plant) in $\frac{1}{4}$ inch dice.
Heat the oil in a pan, add the aubergine (egg plant) and onion. Cover and fry gently until soft, for about 5 minutes. Stir in the flour, then add the remaining ingredients for the filling and bring to boiling point.
Put the halved peppers in a shallow ovenproof dish. Fill with the mixture and cover with foil. Bake at 350°F, Gas Mark 4 for about 10 minutes or until the peppers are soft.
Serves 4

Cauliflower Soup

Soupe au choufleur

2 oz. ($\frac{1}{4}$ cup) butter
1 large onion, sliced
1 garlic clove, crushed
1 medium cauliflower, in
    sprigs
$1\frac{3}{4}$ pints ($4\frac{1}{2}$ cups) chicken
    stock
salt

pepper
4 tablespoons (5T) thin
    (coffee) cream

Garnish:
2 slices toast
1 tablespoon ($1\frac{1}{4}$T) chopped
    parsley

Heat the butter in a large, heavy pan. Add the onion and garlic and fry slowly until soft. Add the cauliflower, water and stock cubes then cover and simmer for 1 hour.
Sieve the soup or purée in a blender. Return it to the pan and check seasoning. Stir in the cream and re-heat the soup almost to simmering point.
Cut the bread in $\frac{1}{2}$-inch cubes and scatter on top of the soup with the parsley just before serving.
Serves 6

Garlic Bread

Pain à l'ail

1 French loaf
2 oz. ($\frac{1}{4}$ cup) butter
1 garlic clove, crushed

1 tablespoon ($1\frac{1}{4}$T) chopped
    parsley

Cut the loaf in 1-inch slices, almost through to the bottom crust. Blend together the remaining ingredients. Spread the mixture between the slices of bread.
Wrap the loaf in foil and cook at 425°F, Gas Mark 7 for 15-20 minutes. Serve hot, divided in slices.
Serves 6

Mushroom Cream Soup

Potage crème de champignons

2 tablespoons (2½T) cooking oil
1 oz. (2T) butter
2 onions, finely chopped
¼ lb. (1¼ cups) mushrooms, finely chopped
3 tablespoons (3¾T) flour
1¼ pints (3 cups) beef stock

¼ pint thin (coffee) cream
salt
pepper
pinch of grated nutmeg
little thick (heavy) cream
1 tablespoon (1¼T) chopped parsley

Heat the oil in a pan, then add the butter. Add the onions and cook until tender, then add the mushrooms and cook for 3 minutes.

Blend in the flour and cook for 1 minute. Gradually add the stock, stirring. Bring to the boil then simmer for about 5 minutes until thick and smooth.

Add the thin cream, seasoning and nutmeg and simmer for 3 minutes. Finally stir in the thick cream and parsley.

Serves 4

Tomato Herb Soup

Soupe aux tomates et aux herbes

½ oz. (1T) butter
1 onion, sliced
1 tablespoon (1¼T) flour
1¼ pints (3 cups) chicken stock
1 blade of mace
6 peppercorns
1 clove
½ teaspoon salt

½ teaspoon castor (superfine) sugar
1 teaspoon paprika
½ teaspoon dried marjoram
1 bay leaf
2-3 sprigs parsley
1 lb. ripe tomatoes, quartered or 16 oz. can (2 cups) tomatoes

12

Melt the butter, add the onion and fry slowly until soft, then blend in the flour and stock and bring to the boil, stirring. Add the rest of the ingredients. Simmer for 30 minutes. Sieve or purée the soup then bring it back to the boil. Check the seasoning before serving.
Serves 4

Bouillabaisse

3 lb. fish to include:
mackerel
plaice (flounder)
whiting
rock salmon (rockfish)
1 cooked crab (optional)
1 small, split lobster tail or
  crawfish tail
$\frac{1}{2}$ pint (1 cup) cooked prawns
  (shrimp)
few cooked mussels
4 tablespoons (5T) olive oil

2 onions, chopped
1 leek, sliced
2 pints (5 cups) fish liquor
4 tomatoes, skinned,
  de-seeded and chopped
$\frac{1}{4}$ teaspoon dried fennel
$\frac{1}{8}$ teaspoon powdered saffron
1 bay leaf
3 sprigs parsley
salt, pepper
6-8 slices French bread

Ask the fishmonger to fillet and skin the mackerel, plaice, whiting and rock salmon but keep the skin and bones for stock. Prepare the crab, if used, and the lobster or crawfish tail. Shell the prawns but keep the mussels in their shells. Put the skin, bones and shells from the fish and shellfish in a pan with $2\frac{1}{2}$ pints (6 cups) water. Bring to the boil and simmer for 20 minutes, then strain off the fish liquor.
Heat the oil in a large pan, add the onion and leek and fry slowly until soft but not coloured. Add the mackerel and plaice, cut in chunks, to the pan and cook gently for 10 minutes, then add the remaining fish, in chunks, fish liquor and all other ingredients except the French bread. Simmer for about 10 minutes until the fish is cooked.
Check the seasoning, discard the bay leaf and parsley. Put the bread in a tureen and pour in the fish mixture.
Serves 6-8

French Onion Soup

Soupe à l'oignon

½ lb. onions, sliced
1 oz. (2T) butter
1 teaspoon castor (superfine)
   sugar
1 tablespoon (1¼T) flour
1½ pints (3¾ cups) beef stock

salt
pepper
4 slices French bread
2 oz. (½ cup) grated Gruyère
   cheese

Brown the onions slowly in the butter. Add the sugar and cook for a few minutes. Add the flour and cook for 1 minute. Add the stock and bring to the boil, stirring. Simmer 20 minutes then add salt and pepper if necessary.
Toast one side of the bread then sprinkle cheese on the untoasted side. Grill until the cheese has melted. Put a slice of bread in each soup bowl and pour the soup on top.
Serves 4

Smoked Mackerel Paté

Pâté de maquereaux fumés
Smoked mackerel can be bought at a large fishmongers or delicatessen. The pâté keeps well in a home freezer.

2 smoked mackerel, skinned
   and boned
3 oz. cream cheese spread
juice of ½ lemon

10 oz. (1¼ cups) butter, melted
salt
pepper

Purée the mackerel in a blender, or mash well with a fork. Gradually add the remaining ingredients and blend until smooth, or mash the mackerel with the cream cheese and then add the other ingredients.
Turn into small ramekins and chill before serving.
Serves 6

Fresh Herb Paté

Pâté aux fines herbes
Make this the day before it is needed so that the flavours blend well.

6 oz. ($\frac{3}{4}$ cup) rich cream cheese
$\frac{1}{4}$ pint ($\frac{1}{2}$ cup + 2T) thick (heavy) cream, lightly whipped
$\frac{1}{2}$ teaspoon freshly chopped thyme
$\frac{1}{2}$ teaspoon freshly chopped dill
1 teaspoon freshly chopped chives
salt
pepper

Blend together the cheese and cream. Stir in the herbs and seasoning. Turn into a $\frac{3}{4}$ pint (2 cups) dish and chill before serving. Serve with crisp biscuits.
Serves 4 as a starter

Brandade of Kipper

Brandade de harengs fumés
A smooth smoked fish pâté

2 large kippers
$1\frac{1}{2}$ oz. (3T) butter
2 teaspoons lemon juice
5 tablespoons ($6\frac{1}{4}$T) thin (coffee) cream
5 tablespoons ($6\frac{1}{4}$T) thick (heavy) cream, lightly whipped
salt
pepper

Dot the kippers with butter and grill (broil) for 10 minutes. Reserve any butter and juices and skin and bone the fish. Purée the kippers in a blender with the juices, or mash with a fork until smooth. When the paste is cold, stir in lemon juice and single cream. Mix until smooth then fold in the double cream. Check the seasoning, turn into 6 individual ramekins and chill until 1 hour before the meal. Serve with hot toast and butter.
Serves 6

Mussels Marinière

Moules à la marinière
When buying mussels, allow 1½ pints (4 cups) per person. Take care not to overcook them. They only take a few minutes, just until the shells are open.

6 pints (15 cups) fresh
   mussels
1 oz. (2T) butter
4 small onions, chopped
4 parsley stalks
2 sprigs fresh thyme or
   ¼ teaspoon dried thyme
1 bay leaf
freshly ground black
   pepper

½ pint (1¼ cups) dry white
   wine
salt
chopped parsley

Beurre Manié:
1 oz. (2T) butter, blended
   with 1 tablespoon (1¼T)
   flour

Scrape and clean each mussel with a strong knife, removing every trace of seaweed, mud and beard. Wash very well and discard any mussels which do not close tightly.

Melt the butter in a large pan, add the onions and fry until soft but not coloured. Add the herbs, pepper and wine and then the mussels. Cover with a tightly fitting lid and cook quickly, shaking the pan constantly, until the mussels open – about 5 to 6 minutes. Lift the mussels out of the pan, discard the empty half of each shell and keep the rest hot in a covered serving dish.

Reduce the cooking liquor to about ½ pint (1¼ cups). Remove the fresh thyme, parsley stalks and bay leaf. Drop the butter and flour mixture into the simmering stock a teaspoon at a time and whisk until the stock is smooth and thickened. Check seasoning.

Pour the sauce over the mussels and scatter with plenty of chopped parsley. Serve with French bread and butter or garlic bread, see page 14.

Finger bowls are a help as picking up mussels is a messy process. You also need a dish for the empty shells.
Serves 4

Eggs in Consommé

Oeufs en gelée

15 oz. can consommé
4 teaspoons powdered
  gelatine

6 small eggs
4 oz. pâté de foie truffé

Put the consommé and gelatine in a pan, leave for 2 minutes then heat gently, without boiling, until the gelatine has dissolved. Cool the mixture.

Soft boil the eggs for 6 minutes then remove the shells carefully and put the eggs in cold water.

Pour $\frac{1}{4}$-inch of consommé into six individual ramekin dishes and leave in a cold place to set. Put an egg in each ramekin and pour over sufficient consommé just to cover. Leave again until set. Spread a layer of pâté on top of each ramekin and leave in a cold place until needed.

Just before serving, turn them out and serve with warm French bread.

Serves 6

Pâté Maison

$\frac{3}{4}$ lb. smoked bacon joint,
  boned and rolled
1 tablespoon ($1\frac{1}{4}$T) clear
  honey
2 teaspoons soft brown sugar
8 cloves
6 peppercorns
$\frac{1}{8}$ teaspoon dried thyme
1 small bay leaf
$\frac{1}{2}$ lb. pigs' liver
1 slice brown bread, with
  crusts removed
$\frac{1}{4}$ lb. pork sausage meat

2 oz. ($\frac{1}{4}$ cup) lard, melted
1 small garlic clove, crushed
grated rind of $\frac{1}{2}$ lemon
1 onion, chopped
$\frac{1}{8}$ teaspoon ground allspice
$\frac{1}{8}$ teaspoon ground nutmeg
$\frac{1}{2}$ teaspoon salt
$\frac{1}{8}$ teaspoon pepper
1 egg
1-2 tablespoons ($1\frac{1}{4}$-$2\frac{1}{2}$T) dry
  sherry
1 large lemon or 5 rashers of
  bacon

Put the bacon in a pan with the honey, sugar, cloves, peppercorns, herbs and sufficient water just to cover. Cover with a lid, bring to boiling point and simmer for 35 minutes then remove the bacon from the pan and take off the rind. Mince the bacon, liver and bread finely then blend with all the other ingredients except the whole lemon.
Slice the lemon very thinly and use to line the base and sides of a greased 2 pint (5 cup) round or oval ovenproof casserole (if preferred, line with rashers of bacon). Fill with the pâté, cover with a lid, or foil, and place in a meat tin, half filled with hot water. Cook at 325°F, Gas Mark 3 for 2 hours. Allow to cool completely before serving.
Serves 6

Eggs Mornay

Oeufs à la mornay

4 eggs
1 oz. (2T) butter
1 oz. (4T) flour
$\frac{1}{4}$ pint ($1\frac{1}{4}$ cups) milk
2 oz. ($\frac{1}{2}$ cup) Gruyère cheese, grated

1 oz. ($\frac{1}{4}$ cup) Parmesan cheese, grated
$\frac{1}{2}$ teaspoon made mustard
salt
pepper

Boil the eggs for only 8 minutes so they are not completely hard. Cool under running cold water. Remove the shells carefully.
Melt the butter in a pan, add the flour and cook for 1 minute. Stir in the milk and bring to boiling point, stirring constantly. Simmer for 2 minutes, remove the pan from the heat and stir in most of the cheese. Add mustard and plenty of seasoning.
Cut the eggs in half lengthways. Arrange in an ovenproof serving dish. Spoon over the sauce. Sprinkle with the remaining cheese. Brown under the grill (broiler). Serve with a green salad and toast.
Serves 4

Cheese Soufflé

Soufflé au fromage

If you are making this soufflé for guests, get it to the white sauce stage then add the yolks and cheese. Fifty minutes or so before serving whisk the egg whites until stiff and fold into the mixture. Turn into the prepared soufflé dish and cook as below

3 oz. (6T) butter
2 oz. ($\frac{1}{2}$ cup) plain (all-purpose) flour
$\frac{1}{2}$ pint (1$\frac{1}{4}$ cups) milk
1 oz. ($\frac{1}{4}$ cup) grated Parmesan cheese

3 oz. ($\frac{3}{4}$ cup) Gruyère cheese, grated
salt
pepper
1 teaspoon Dijon mustard
3 large eggs, separated

Butter a 2 pint (5 cup) soufflé dish. Melt the butter in a pan. Stir in the flour, then blend in the milk. Bring to the boil, stirring constantly, then simmer for 3 minutes. Remove the pan from the heat and beat in the cheese, seasoning and mustard. Beat in the egg yolks, one at a time.

Whisk the egg whites until stiff, then fold into the cheese mixture. Turn into the prepared dish and cook at 375°F, Gas Mark 5 for about 45 minutes, until the soufflé is well risen and the top is set and slightly crusty. Serve at once.

Serves 4

Crudités

This is a selection of prepared, raw vegetables served with Aioli, a garlic flavoured mayonnaise. Try some of the following:

Cauliflower, broken in small sprigs
Cucumber, peeled and cut in 2 inch long fingers
Radishes, washed and left whole
Carrots, peeled and cut in fingers
Celery, each stalk halved lengthways and cut in fingers
Chicory, divided in leaves
Green pepper, de-seeded and cut in strips
Tomatoes, quartered and seeded
See page 66 for Aïoli recipe

French Dressed Globe Artichokes

Artichauts à la vinaigrette

Dressing:
1 teaspoon castor (superfine) sugar
$\frac{1}{2}$ teaspoon salt
$\frac{1}{8}$ teaspoon pepper
1 teaspoon chopped chives
5 tablespoons ($6\frac{1}{4}$T) olive oil
2 tablespoons ($2\frac{1}{2}$T) wine vinegar
$\frac{1}{4}$ teaspoon dried basil

1 lb. firm tomatoes, skinned
2 × 12 oz. cans globe artichoke hearts, drained
1 tablespoon ($1\frac{1}{4}$T) chopped parsley
brown bread and butter

Blend together all the dressing ingredients.
Slice the tomatoes thinly, then arrange them on small, individual plates. Arrange the artichoke hearts on top and spoon over the dressing.
Leave in a cold place until just before serving. Scatter with parsley and serve with thinly sliced bread and butter.
Serves 6

Pissaladière

Rich shortcrust pastry:
5 oz. (1¼ cups) plain flour
½ teaspoon salt
2½ oz. (5T) butter
1 egg
Filling:
1 tablespoon (1¼T) olive oil
1 oz. (2T) butter
1½ lb. onions, finely sliced

½ teaspoon salt
⅛ teaspoon pepper
⅛ teaspoon ground nutmeg
3 egg yolks
3 tablespoons (3¾T) milk
¼ lb. (½ cup) cream cheese
Garnish:
about 16 anchovy fillets
16 black olives

Make the pastry in the usual way, adding sufficient egg to bind the mixture together. Wrap it in foil and chill for 2 hours. Heat the oil in a pan, add the butter and cook the onions, slowly, covered, for 30 minutes until soft and pale golden, then add seasoning and nutmeg and put on one side. Use the pastry to line a shallow 9-inch fluted flan tin placed on a baking tray. Line with greaseproof paper and baking beans, or foil, and bake 'blind' at 400°F, Gas Mark 6 for 20 minutes. Remove the beans and paper, or foil.
Blend together the egg yolks, milk and cheese, then mix with the onion. Pour the filling into the pastry case and cook at 350°F, Gas Mark 4 for 20 minutes or until just set. Arrange the anchovy fillets in a lattice on top of the filling with the black olives, then cook for a further 10 minutes.
Serves 6

Baked Eggs with Aubergines

Oeufs cocotte aux aubergines

$\frac{1}{2}$ lb. aubergines (egg plant)
salt
4 tablespoons (5T) salad oil
1 large onion, sliced
3 tomatoes, skinned and
   sliced

seasoning
6 eggs
6 tablespoons ($7\frac{1}{2}$T) thin
   (coffee) cream

Cut the aubergines (egg plant) in $\frac{1}{2}$ inch dice, put on a plate and sprinkle thickly with salt. Leave for 15 minutes, then rinse in cold water and dry on kitchen paper.

Heat the oil in a pan, add the aubergines (egg plant) and onion, cover and cook gently for 20 minutes. Add the tomatoes and cook for a further 10 minutes.

Remove the pan from the heat, check the seasoning and divide between 6 individual $\frac{1}{4}$ pint ($\frac{1}{2}$ cup capacity) ovenproof dishes. Break an egg into each dish and spoon over the cream. Place the dishes on a baking tray and cook at 350°F, Gas Mark 4 for about 10 minutes or until the eggs are just set.

Serves 6

Eggs in Curry Sauce

Oeufs à l'indienne

6 hard-boiled eggs
$\frac{1}{2}$ lettuce, shredded
$\frac{1}{2}$ pint ($1\frac{1}{4}$ cups) mayonnaise,
   see page 87.
2 teaspoons lemon juice
1 teaspoon curry powder

1 tablespoon ($1\frac{1}{4}$T) mango
   chutney, chopped
pinch of chilli pepper
salt
pepper

28

Shell the eggs and cut in half lengthways. Arrange, cut side down, on six small plates with shredded lettuce.
Blend together the remaining ingredients and check the seasoning. Spoon mayonnaise over the eggs.
Serves 6

Mushroom Vols Au Vent

Vol-au-vent de champignons

6 oz. puff pastry, made with
  6 oz. (1½ cups) flour, 6 oz.
  (¾ cup) butter

or

11 oz. packet frozen puff pastry
1 egg blended with 1
  tablespoon (1¼T) water

Filling:
1½ oz. (3T) butter
6 oz. (2 cups) mushrooms,
  sliced
1 oz. (4T) flour
½ pint (1¼ cups) milk
salt
pepper

Roll the pastry out ¼ inch thick, on a well floured board. Cut six 3 inch circles with a pastry cutter. Make a smaller cut ¼ inch inside each case but do not cut completely through the pastry. Place on an ungreased baking tray and chill in the refrigerator for 30 minutes.
Brush the tops of the cases with egg glaze and bake at 400°F, Gas Mark 6 for 20 minutes, or until well risen and golden brown. Remove from the baking sheet and cool on a wire rack. Carefully remove the 'lids' with a sharp knife and scoop out any uncooked mixture.
Melt the butter for the filling in a pan. Add the mushrooms, cover and cook for 2 minutes. Blend in the flour and cook for 1 minute. Blend in the milk and bring to the boil then simmer for 2 minutes. Season well with salt and pepper.
Fill the prepared cases with the mixture and replace the lids. Re-heat at 400°F, Gas Mark 6 for 10-15 minutes.
Serves 6 as a starter

Individual Quiches

Petites quiches
These small tarts make a substantial beginning to a summer dinner party.

Pastry:
6 oz. shortcrust pastry made
   with 6 oz. (1½ cups) flour,
   etc. see page 36.

Filling:
4 oz. shelled shrimps or
   prawns

1 egg
4 oz. carton (½ cup) thin
   (coffee) cream
1 oz. (¼ cup) Cheddar cheese,
   finely grated
¼ teaspoon salt
⅛ teaspoon pepper

Use the pastry to line 12 individual patty tins. Bake 'blind' at
400°F, Gas Mark 6 for 7 minutes. Remove the paper and
baking beans, or foil.
Divide the shrimps or prawns between the pastry cases. Blend
together the remaining ingredients and spoon into the cases.
Bake at 350°F, Gas Mark 4 for about 20 minutes or until the
filling is pale golden and lightly set.
Serves 6 as a starter

Shortcrust Pastry

Pâté brisée

8 oz. (2 cups) plain (all-
   purpose) flour
½ teaspoon salt

2 oz. (¼ cup) butter
2 oz. (¼ cup) lard
about 8 teaspoons cold water

Sift the flour and salt into a bowl. Cut the fats in small pieces
then rub into the flour with the tips of the fingers until the
mixture resembles fine breadcrumbs. Add enough water to
mix to a firm dough. Roll out thinly on a floured board and
use as required.

TOP OF THE BILL OF FARE

Those with modest appetites may willingly forego the third course. They may even dispense with the first. But the main course is always the star turn. The art of French cookery is typified in the following recipes, which make full use of wine, herbs and garlic.

Beef Fillet in Pastry

Filet de boeuf en croûte
When entertaining, the prepared dish can be left in the refrigerator for up to 12 hours before cooking.

2 oz. ($\frac{1}{4}$ cup) butter
1$\frac{1}{2}$ lb. fillet of beef
1 garlic clove, crushed
$\frac{1}{4}$ lb. (1$\frac{1}{3}$ cups) mushrooms, sliced
4 tablespoons (5T) Madeira wine

$\frac{1}{2}$ teaspoon salt
$\frac{1}{8}$ teaspoon pepper
4 oz. puff pastry, made with 4 oz. (1 cup) flour, etc. or 7$\frac{1}{2}$ oz. frozen puff pastry
milk for glazing

Melt the butter in a pan, add the beef and garlic and fry quickly for 15 minutes (or 10 minutes for a rare centre to the beef, 25 minutes for a well-done fillet), turning on all sides. Remove the beef from the pan, add the mushrooms and cook until soft. Put the Madeira in the pan and simmer until the liquid has reduced by half. Remove the pan from the heat and add seasoning.

Roll out the pastry to a rectangle, about 9 by 12 inches. This will vary according to the size of the fillet. Put the beef in the centre of the pastry with the mushrooms on top and spoon over the sauce. Fold over the pastry, moisten the edges and seal firmly with the fold on top so that juices do not run out. Chill for 30 minutes.

Place on a baking tray, glaze with milk and cook at 400°F, Gas Mark 6 for about 25 minutes until the pastry is golden.
Serves 4-6

Pot Roast

Boeuf à la mode
There is no need to use prime beef for this recipe.

$\frac{1}{2}$ pint (1$\frac{1}{4}$ cups) beef stock
4 × 5 oz. pieces rump steak
$\frac{1}{4}$ pint ($\frac{1}{2}$ cup + 2T) red wine
1 small onion, finely chopped
1 teaspoon mixed dried herbs
1 oz. (2T) lard or dripping
8 baby onions
1$\frac{1}{2}$ tablespoons (2T) flour

$\frac{1}{4}$ lb. carrots, sliced with a
    fluted chip cutter
salt
pepper
few drops of gravy browning
1 tablespoon (1$\frac{1}{4}$T) chopped
    parsley

Put the steak in a dish with the stock, wine, chopped onion
and herbs and marinate for at least 2 hours, turning
occasionally. Drain the meat, reserving the marinade. Melt the
lard or dripping in a pan, add the meat and baby onions and
fry until browned. Transfer to an ovenproof casserole.
Add the flour to the fat remaining in the pan and fry gently
until browned. Stir in the marinade and bring to the boil. Add
to the casserole with the carrots, seasoning and gravy
browning. Cover and cook at 300°F, Gas Mark 2 for 1$\frac{1}{2}$ hours
or until the meat is tender. Serve the meat in a hot dish with
the vegetables arranged around it. Garnish with chopped
parsley just before serving.
Serves 4

POT ROAST *(Photograph: Argentine Beef Bureau)*

Burgundy Beef

Boeuf bourguignonne

$1\frac{1}{2}$ lb. chuck steak
1 oz. (2T) bacon fat
6 oz. unsmoked streaky
   bacon, rinded and cut in
   $\frac{1}{2}$ inch wide strips
$\frac{1}{2}$ oz. (2T) flour
$\frac{1}{2}$ pint beef stock
$\frac{1}{4}$ pint red wine
1 bay leaf

$\frac{1}{2}$ level teaspoon dried mixed
   herbs
sprig of parsley
about $\frac{1}{2}$ level teaspoon salt
$\frac{1}{8}$ level teaspoon pepper
$\frac{1}{4}$ lb. small, even-sized onions,
   peeled
2 oz. button mushrooms

Cut the steak into $1\frac{1}{2}$ inch squares. Melt the bacon fat in a
fairly large pan and fry the bacon for a few minutes until it
begins to turn brown. Lift the bacon out of the pan and into a
3-pint (8-cup) casserole and then fry the steak in fat remaining
in the pan until it is brown all over.

Add the steak to the bacon in the casserole and pour off all but
2 tablespoons ($2\frac{1}{2}$T) of the fat. Blend the flour with the fat and
continue to cook until it has browned. Remove the pan from
the heat and stir in stock and wine. Return the pan to the heat
and bring the liquor to boiling point. Simmer until it has
thickened.

Add the bay leaf, herbs, parsley and seasoning, adding only a
little of the salt, as the bacon may be salty. Pour the liquor
over the meat, cover the casserole and simmer gently in the
oven at 325°F, Gas Mark 3 for $1\frac{1}{2}$ hours.

Add the onions and mushrooms to the casserole and cook it
for a further hour or until the meat is really tender. Check
seasoning and add more salt and pepper if necessary. Skim off
any fat on the surface.

Serves 6

Pepperpot Beef

Pot-au-feu piquant

1 oz. (4T) flour
1 teaspoon salt
$\frac{1}{8}$ teaspoon pepper
$\frac{1}{2}$ teaspoon ground ginger
2 lb. braising beef, in 1 inch
   cubes
2 oz. ($\frac{1}{4}$ cup) lard or dripping
1 small red pepper, sliced
15 oz. can red kidney beans,
   drained

Sauce:
1 teaspoon chilli sauce
8 oz. can tomatoes
$\frac{1}{4}$ lb. ($1\frac{1}{4}$ cups) mushrooms,
   sliced
1 tablespoon ($1\frac{1}{4}$T)
   Worcestershire sauce
2 tablespoons ($2\frac{1}{2}$T) soft brown
   sugar
2 tablespoons ($2\frac{1}{2}$T) wine
   vinegar
2 garlic cloves, crushed
1 bay leaf

Mix together the flour, seasonings and ginger and use to coat the beef. Heat the lard in a large pan, add the beef and fry quickly until browned, turning once. Drain on kitchen paper then transfer to a 3 pint ($8\frac{1}{2}$ cups) ovenproof dish.
Combine all the ingredients for the sauce and pour over the meat. Cover and cook at 325°F, Gas Mark 3 for about 2 hours or until the meat is tender. Add the red pepper and kidney beans 30 minutes before the end of the cooking time.
Serves 6

Pork Fillet in Wine

Filet de porc chasseur

2 lb. pork fillet (tenderloin)
2 tablespoons (2½T) oil
2 oz. (4T) butter
½ lb. onions, chopped
½ lb. (2⅔ cups) button
   mushrooms

2 tablespoons (2½T) flour
½ pint (1¼ cups) beef stock
¼ pint (½ cup) white wine
salt
pepper

Cut the pork in 1½-inch pieces. Heat the oil in a pan, brown the pork quickly in the oil then remove from the pan. Heat the butter in the pan, add the onions and cook slowly until soft. Add the mushrooms.

Blend in the flour, stock and wine. Bring to the boil then simmer for 2-3 minutes. Replace the pork in the pan and season with salt and pepper. Cover and simmer for 40-50 minutes, until the pork is tender.

Serves 6

Pork in Cream Sauce

Côtelettes de porc à la crème

4 pork chops
salt
ground black pepper
1½ oz. (3T) butter
½ lb. (2⅔ cups) mushrooms,
  sliced

2 tablespoons (2½T) flour
½ pint (1¼ cups) dry white
  wine
pinch dried mixed herbs
¼ pint (½ cup + 2T) thin
  (coffee) cream

Season the chops with salt and pepper. Cook under a medium grill (broiler) for 10 minutes on a piece of foil, turning once, until crisp and brown. Save the juices on the foil. Place the chops on a serving dish and keep hot.

Melt the butter in a pan, add the mushrooms and fry gently for about 5 minutes until soft. Stir in the flour and cook for 1 minute. Blend in the juices from the foil, wine and herbs. Simmer for 2 minutes, stirring all the time. Add the cream and check the seasoning. Reheat almost to boiling point.

Pour the sauce over the chops. Serve with buttered noodles and grilled tomatoes.

Serves 4

Bayonne Lamb

Collier de mouton à la bayonne
A really economical French country stew.

2 lb. middle neck of lamb,
  chopped
2 onions, cut in wedges
2 large carrots, sliced
4 baby turnips, peeled and
  kept whole
1 bay leaf
1 tablespoon (1¼T) lemon
  juice
salt

pepper
2 pints (5 cups) water
¼ lb. (1⅓ cups) small
  mushrooms, sliced
1¼ oz. (3T) butter
1½ oz. (6T) flour
1 egg yolk
4 oz. carton (½ cup) thin
  (coffee) cream

Put the lamb in a pan with the onions, carrots, turnips, bay leaf, lemon juice, seasoning and water. Bring to boiling point, cover and simmer for 1½ hours or until tender. Twenty minutes before the end of the cooking time add the mushrooms. Arrange the lamb and vegetables in a serving dish and keep hot.
Reduce the cooking liquor to 1 pint (2½ cups) by boiling rapidly. Make a roux with the butter and flour, add the cooking liquor and simmer for 5 minutes. Add more seasoning if necessary. Blend together the egg yolk and cream and add a little of the sauce. Return this mixture to the pan and re-heat but do not boil. Pour the sauce over the meat and vegetables.
Serves 4

Lamb in Pastry

Gigot d'agneau en croûte
This is a delicious way of cooking lamb. When you serve the joint, cut and lift the pastry off in portions and then carve the meat as you would normally. Serve with a rich gravy.

4 lb. leg of lamb
2 oz. ($\frac{1}{4}$ cup) butter
salt
pepper
For the pastry:
10 oz. ($2\frac{1}{2}$ cups) plain
   (all-purpose) flour

$\frac{3}{4}$ teaspoon salt
$2\frac{1}{2}$ oz. (5T) butter
$2\frac{1}{2}$ oz. (5T) lard
about 10 teaspoons water
Glaze:
1 egg, beaten with
1 teaspoon water

Have the bone of the joint cut short and trim off any excess fat. Rub the joint with the butter and sprinkle it with salt and pepper. Place it in the meat tin and roast it at 425°F, Gas Mark 7 for 75 minutes. Remove it from the oven and leave to cool. Sift the flour and salt into a bowl. Add the fats and rub in until the mixture resembles fine breadcrumbs. Add enough of the water to make a firm dough. Roll out the pastry to form a rectangle large enough to cover the lamb.
Wrap the lamb in the pastry with the joint underneath. Return the joint to the meat tin and decorate it with small leaves made from the pastry trimmings. Prick the pastry all over with a knife. Brush the pastry with beaten egg and bake the joint at 375°F, Gas Mark 5 for a further 45 minutes.
Serves 8

ROAST LAMB IN PASTRY *(Photograph: New Zealand Lamb Information Bureau)*

Veal Casserole

Blanquette de veau

1½ lb. boned shoulder veal, in 1½ inch pieces
2 onions, quartered
2 large carrots, quartered
3 bay leaves
sprig of parsley
1 tablespoon (1¼T) lemon juice
salt
pepper

2 pints (5 cups) water
6 oz. (2 cups) button mushrooms
1½ oz. (3T) butter
1½ oz. (6T) flour
1 egg yolk
¼ pint (½ cup + 2T) thin (coffee) cream

Put the veal in a pan, cover with cold water and bring to the boil. Drain the veal and rinse off any scum. Put the veal pieces in a pan with the onions, carrots, bay leaves, parsley, lemon juice, seasoning and water. Bring to boiling point, cover and simmer for 1½ hours or until the veal is tender. Half an hour before the end of the cooking time add the mushrooms. Arrange the veal and vegetables in a serving dish and keep hot.

Make a roux with the butter and flour. Reduce the cooking liquor to 1 pint (2½ cups) by boiling rapidly, then blend with the roux and simmer for 5 minutes. Check the seasoning. Blend together the egg yolk and cream. Add a little of the sauce. Return the egg mixture to the pan and re-heat but do not boil. Pour the sauce over the meat and vegetables.

Serves 4

Veal Birds

Paupiettes de veau
Chicken breasts, boned out and beaten, may be used instead of veal.

1 lb. veal fillet (scallops) in thin slices

2 rashers bacon, rinded and chopped

1 tablespoon (1¼T) chopped parsley

1 small garlic clove, crushed

2 oz. (1 cup) fresh white breadcrumbs

1 egg

1 oz. butter (2T)

1 tablespoon (1¼T) flour

¼ pint (½ cup + 2T) water or stock

¼ pint (½ cup + 2T) dry white wine

salt

pepper

¼ lb. (1⅓ cups) mushrooms, halved

4 tomatoes, peeled and quartered

few stuffed green olives

Beat the veal on a wooden board with a rolling pin until very thin. Mix together the bacon, parsley, garlic, breadcrumbs and egg and use to stuff the slices of veal. Roll each slice tightly and tie with fine string. Melt the butter in a pan, add the veal and fry quickly until browned. Remove the veal from the pan and place in a 2½ pint (6-cup) ovenproof dish.

Add the flour to the pan and cook for 1 minute. Stir in the water or stock and wine, bring to the boil, add seasoning and pour over the veal. Cover and cook at 325°F, Gas Mark 3 for 1 hour. Half an hour before the end of the cooking time add the remaining ingredients.

Serves 4

Chicken in Wine

Coq au vin

3-4 lb. boiling or roasting
   chicken
$1\frac{1}{2}$ oz. (3T) butter
1 tablespoon ($1\frac{1}{4}$T) salad oil
4 oz. piece smoked streaky
   bacon, cubed
12 baby onions
2 sticks celery, finely
   chopped
6 oz. (2 cups) mushrooms,
   quartered

1 garlic clove, crushed
2 tablespoons ($2\frac{1}{2}$T) flour
$\frac{3}{4}$ pint (2 cups) red Burgundy
$\frac{1}{4}$ pint ($\frac{1}{2}$ cup + 2T) water
1 bay leaf
1 sprig fresh thyme or
   $\frac{1}{4}$ teaspoon dried thyme
salt
pepper
the chicken giblets, washed
small triangles of fried bread

Wash and dry the chicken and cut into 6 joints. Melt 1 oz.
(2T) butter in a pan with the oil and fry the bacon cubes until
golden brown. Remove the bacon from the pan and drain on
kitchen paper. Fry the chicken until brown, turning once.
Put the joints, with the bacon, into a 3 pint (8 cup) ovenproof
casserole. Fry the onions with the celery in the fat remaining
in the pan until soft, then add to the casserole. Melt the
remaining butter in the pan, add the mushrooms and cook for
2 minutes, then put to one side, on kitchen paper.
Blend the garlic and flour with the fat remaining in the pan.
Cook gently until browned, stirring frequently. Add the wine,
water, herbs and seasoning to taste. Simmer until the mixture
has thickened. Pour over the chicken joints in the casserole
and add the giblets. Cover and cook at 325°F, Gas Mark 3 for
$1\frac{1}{2}$-4 hours, depending on the size of the bird and whether it
is a boiling or roasting chicken.
When almost tender remove the giblets and bay leaf from the
casserole. Stir in the mushrooms and cook for a further 10
minutes. Skim off any excess fat with absorbent kitchen paper.
Check the seasoning and garnish with fried bread triangles
before serving.
Serves 6

Tarragon Chicken

Poulet à l'estragon

$3\frac{1}{2}$-4 lb. chicken
$\frac{1}{2}$ lemon
$\frac{1}{2}$ teaspoon salt
$\frac{1}{8}$ teaspoon pepper
$\frac{1}{4}$ teaspoon dried tarragon
3 carrots, quartered
1 onion, quartered
1 bay leaf
2 parsley sprigs
$\frac{3}{4}$ pint (2 cups) chicken stock
6 tablespoons ($7\frac{1}{2}$T) white wine

Sauce:
1 oz. (2T) butter
2 tablespoons ($2\frac{1}{2}$T) flour
$\frac{1}{2}$ teaspoon dried tarragon
2 egg yolks
5 tablespoons ($6\frac{1}{4}$T) thin
  (coffee) cream
salt
pepper

Put the chicken in a pan with the giblets and the first group
of ingredients. Cover and simmer for about $1\frac{1}{4}$ hours or until
tender. Remove the bird from the pan, skin and joint it and,
if liked, remove the bones. Keep the chicken hot.
Strain the cooking liquor into a measuring jug and make it up
to $\frac{3}{4}$ pint (2 cups) with water if necessary. Heat the butter in
a pan, blend in the flour and cook for 1 minute. Add the
chicken liquor and bring to the boil, stirring. Add the tarragon
and simmer for 3 minutes.
Blend together the egg yolks and cream. Add 4 tablespoons
(5T) sauce to the egg mixture then return it to the pan. Check
the seasoning, add the chicken pieces and heat through,
without simmering, for 5 minutes.
Serves 6

Duck with Orange

Canard à l'orange

Watercress and an orange salad – sliced oranges in a dressing made from orange juice, wine vinegar and oil – are the classic accompaniments for this dish.

1 duckling, about 4½–5 lb.
salt
pepper
1 large orange
2 tablespoons (2½T) clear
   honey
few drops of gravy browning
1 oz. (4T) flour
¼ pint (½ cup + 2T) fresh
   orange juice

¼ pint (½ cup + 2T) red wine
1 tablespoon (1¼T) redcurrant
   jelly

Garnish:
1 orange, thinly sliced
bunch of watercress

Sprinkle the duckling inside and out with salt and pepper. Peel the zest from the orange and cut in thin strips. Discard the pith then divide the orange in segments. Put the segments in the body cavity of the duckling. Put in a meat tin and prick the entire body with a fork. Roast at 325°F, Gas Mark 3 for 2½–3 hours.

Cover the duck neck and giblets with water and cook until tender. Strain and reserve ½ pint (1¼ cups) stock.

Remove the duckling from the oven and raise the oven temperature to 350°F, Gas Mark 4. Pour off the dripping. Brush the duckling with the honey, mixed with gravy browning. Roast for a further 30 minutes.

Put 4 tablespoons (5T) dripping in a pan then blend in the flour. Stir in the stock, orange juice, wine and reserved strips of orange zest. Simmer until the sauce has reduced by a third. Add and dissolve the redcurrant jelly.

Put the duck on a hot serving dish. Spoon over a little of the sauce and serve the rest separately. Put the orange segments from the body cavity onto the breast of the duck and garnish with halved orange slices and sprigs of watercress.

Serves 4

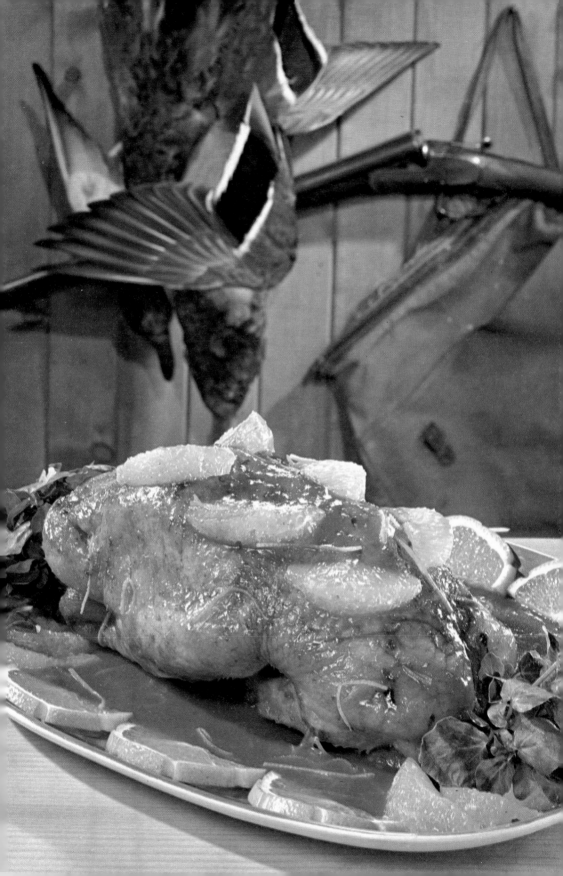

Sauté of Cod

Cabillaud à la mistral

1 oz. (2T) butter
4 cod cutlets
1 onion, chopped
1 garlic clove, crushed
6 oz. (2 cups) mushrooms, sliced
½ lb. tomatoes, skinned, seeded and diced

5 tablespoons (6¼T) dry white wine
salt
pepper
1 tablespoon (1¼T) browned breadcrumbs
1 tablespoon (1¼T) chopped parsley

Melt the butter in a frying pan, add the cod cutlets and cook gently for 10 minutes, turning once. Transfer the fish to a serving dish and keep hot.
Add the onion and garlic to the pan and cook slowly until the onion is soft but not coloured. Add the mushrooms and tomatoes and cook for a further 3 minutes. Stir in the wine, bring to the boil and simmer for 5 minutes. Check the seasoning and pour the sauce over the cutlets.
Mix together the breadcrumbs and parsley and scatter over the fish.
Serves 4

Fresh Salmon with Prawns

Saumon aux crevettes
A special summer dish.

2½ lb. tail piece salmon
¼ pint (½ cup + 2T) dry white wine
½ pint (1¼ cups) water
1 bay leaf
2 sprigs parsley
6 peppercorns

Garnish:
1½ teaspoons powdered gelatine
15 oz. can consommé
½ cucumber, thinly sliced
6 oz. (¾ cup) shelled prawns (shrimps)

Put the salmon in a large buttered ovenproof dish with the other ingredients. Cover with a lid, or foil, and cook at 325°F, Gas Mark 3 for about 45 minutes, basting frequently. Remove from the oven and leave to cool in the dish, basting occasionally.

When cold remove the skin. Divide the fish in half by sliding a sharp knife along both sides of the flat backbone. Arrange on a large serving dish, putting a tail at each end of the dish. Put in the refrigerator.

Dissolve the gelatine with the consommé in a pan over gentle heat. Remove the pan from the heat and cool until the consommé has thickened slightly. Arrange the cucumber slices, overlapping slightly, round the edge of the salmon. Put the prawns in the centre, spoon the consommé over the top and chill until set.

Serves 6

Trout with Almonds

Truites aux amandes

2 oz. ($\frac{1}{4}$ cup) butter
2 oz. ($\frac{1}{3}$ cup) blanched
   almonds, shredded
4 trout, cleaned

salt
pepper
few parsley sprigs
4 black olives

Melt the butter in a frying pan, add the almonds and fry gently until golden brown. Remove the almonds from the pan. Meanwhile wash and dry the trout. Remove the fins and part of the tails but leave the heads on. Fry the trout in the butter remaining in the pan, allowing about 5 minutes on each side, according to size. Season to taste.

Arrange the trout on a hot serving dish with a black olive in the mouth of each. Sprinkle with the almonds and pour over the butter from the pan. Garnish with parsley.

Serves 4

Bacon and Onion Quiche

Quiche lorraine

4 oz. shortcrust pastry,
  see page 36

Filling:
1 small onion, chopped
$\frac{1}{2}$ oz. (1T) butter
$\frac{1}{4}$ lb. bacon, rinded

1 egg
$\frac{1}{4}$ pint ($\frac{1}{2}$ cup + 2T) thin
  (coffee) cream
salt
pepper
2 tomatoes, sliced

Use the pastry to line a 7 inch fluted flan ring placed on a
baking tray. Chill in the refrigerator for 10 minutes then bake
'blind' at 425°F, Gas Mark 7 for 15 minutes. Remove from the
oven and discard the paper and baking beans, or foil.
Fry the onion in the butter until soft but not coloured. Chop
the bacon and add to the pan. Fry the onion and bacon until
golden brown. Blend together the egg, cream and seasoning.
Put the onion and bacon in the flan case. Strain the egg
mixture on top. Arrange the tomatoes round the top of the
quiche. Cook at 350°F, Gas Mark 4 for 35 minutes or until the
filling is set.
Serves 4

Sole with Cucumber Sauce

Soles aux concombres

$1\frac{1}{2}$ oz. (3T) butter
12 fillets of lemon sole
juice of $\frac{1}{2}$ lemon
$\frac{1}{8}$ teaspoon freshly ground
   black pepper
1 teaspoon chopped parsley
Sauce:
$\frac{1}{2}$ cucumber, peeled

salt
$\frac{1}{4}$ pint ($\frac{1}{2}$ cup + 2T)
   mayonnaise, see page 87
$\frac{1}{4}$ pint ($\frac{1}{2}$ cup + 2T) thick
   (heavy) cream, lightly
   whipped
juice of $\frac{1}{2}$ lemon
pepper

Use $\frac{1}{2}$ oz. (1T) butter to grease a $1\frac{1}{2}$ pint (4 cup) shallow ovenproof dish. Place the fish in the dish, dot with the remaining butter and add the lemon juice and pepper. Cover with foil and bake at 325°F, Gas Mark 3 for about 25 minutes or until the fish will flake easily.

Cut the cucumber in $\frac{1}{4}$ inch dice, place on a plate, sprinkle thickly with salt and leave for 15 minutes. Rinse the cucumber in cold water, then dry on kitchen paper. Blend together the remaining sauce ingredients, then add the cucumber. Arrange the fish on a hot serving dish, sprinkle with parsley and serve with the sauce.

Serves 6

French Omelette

Omelette

The size of the pan is very important for an omelette. Use a 6-inch pan for two eggs and a 7-inch pan for a three egg quantity.

3 eggs
salt

pepper
$\frac{1}{2}$ oz. (1T) butter

Beat the eggs with a fork until lightly mixed, then beat in the seasoning. Slowly heat a heavy, 7 inch diameter omelette pan until very hot. Add the butter, and as soon as it has melted, pour in the eggs. Using the fork, keep drawing some of the mixture to the middle from the sides of the pan. Cook for $1\frac{1}{2}$ to 2 minutes until soft but not runny. Remove the pan from the heat and, using the fork, fold the omelette away from you but only half over. Tilt the pan over a hot plate. The omelette will slip forward onto the plate, neatly folded.

Serves 1 or 2

Variations

Cheese: add 2 oz. ($\frac{1}{2}$ cup) finely grated cheese to mixture.
Fines herbes: 1 tablespoon ($\frac{1}{2}$T) chopped parsley and a few chopped chives added to the eggs before cooking.
Onion: 1 large onion fried in butter then cooled and added to the egg mixture.
Kidney: Peel, core and chop 2 lambs' kidneys. Fry in a little onion. Pile into the cooked omelette.
Mushroom: 2 oz. ($\frac{5}{8}$ cup) chopped mushrooms fried in butter and added to the cooked omelette.
Shellfish: warm through in a little white sauce and pile into the cooked omelette.

SUPPORTING ROLES: VEGETABLES AND SALADS

In family meals in France and in restaurants which cater mainly for French customers rather than visiting tourists, vegetables or salads are served as a separate course. This enables one to savour the full flavour of the dish in isolation, a point worth remembering if the main course is itself highly flavoured. Among the recipes given here are one or two which could be served as a first course.

French Baked Onions

Oignons rôtis

8 large onions, peeled	salt
2 oz. ($\frac{1}{4}$ cup) butter	freshly ground black pepper

Dot the onions with butter, then season. Wrap each onion in foil and place on a baking tray. Bake at 350°F, Gas Mark 4 for about $1\frac{1}{2}$ hours, until tender.
Serves 4

Duchess Potatoes

Pommes de terre duchesse

1 lb. potatoes	salt
1 egg yolk	pepper
1 oz. (2T) butter	little beaten egg

Peel, boil and mash the potatoes. Beat in the egg yolk, butter and seasoning. Pipe in large rosettes on a baking tray. Brush with beaten egg and bake at 425°F, Gas Mark 7 until golden.

Lyonnaise Potatoes

Pommes de terre lyonnaise

1 lb. potatoes, peeled and
   thinly sliced
1 large onion,
   thinly sliced

2 oz. ($\frac{1}{4}$ cup) butter
salt
pepper
chopped parsley

Blanch the potatoes in boiling water for 1 minute, then drain. Fry the onion in butter for a few minutes, without colouring. Layer the onion, potatoes and seasoning in a buttered 2 pint (5 cup) casserole, finishing with a layer of potatoes. Pour over any butter left in the pan, cover and bake at 400°F, Gas Mark 6 for $1\frac{1}{2}$ hours. Remove the lid for the last 30 minutes to allow the potatoes to brown. Sprinkle with parsley.

Courgette (Zucchini) Fritters

Beignets de courgettes
Serve as a starter with tomato sauce, or as a vegetable.

1 lb. courgettes (zucchini)

Batter:
4 oz. (1 cup)
   plain (all-purpose) flour

$\frac{1}{2}$ teaspoon salt
2 eggs, separated
about $\frac{1}{4}$ pint
   ($\frac{1}{2}$ cup + 2T) milk
oil for deep frying

Cut the courgettes in $\frac{1}{4}$ inch slices. Put the flour and salt in a bowl and blend in the egg yolks. Add sufficient milk to make a coating batter. Whisk the egg whites stiffly and fold into the batter.
Heat the oil in a pan, dip the sliced courgettes in the batter then fry until golden brown. Drain on kitchen paper and serve hot.
Serves 4

Dauphine Potatoes

Pommes de terre dauphine

$1\frac{1}{2}$ oz. (3T) butter
$\frac{1}{4}$ pint ($\frac{1}{2}$ cup + 2T)
   water
2 eggs

$2\frac{1}{2}$ oz. (10T) plain
   (all-purpose) flour
1 lb. basic Duchesse
   potato mixture, see page 58

Make choux paste in the usual way with butter, water, flour
and eggs, see page 89. Beat the uncooked paste into the
Duchesse mixture. Shape in rounds with 2 greased spoons.
Fry in hot fat until golden brown, drain on kitchen tissue and
sprinkle with salt before serving.

Country Fried Potatoes

Pommes de terre paysanne

1 lb. peeled potatoes
2 oz. ($\frac{1}{4}$ cup) butter

1 garlic clove, crushed

Cut the potatoes in $\frac{1}{2}$ inch dice. Fry gently in butter until
golden brown. Add garlic to the pan just before serving and
mix well.

Asparagus

Asperges

1 lb. bundle of asparagus   salt

Trim off the white and brown jagged ends of the asparagus
and cut all the sticks to an average length. Scrape off the
rough skin near the cut end with a sharp knife. Wash well
in cold water.
Bring a large, shallow pan of salted water to the boil, add the
asparagus, cover and simmer for 12 to 15 minutes or until just
tender. Lift out the asparagus carefully and drain.
Serve hot with hollandaise sauce, see page 65, or melted
butter, or cold with French dressing, see page 70.
Serves 2-3

Leeks with Cheese

Poireaux au gratin

4 leeks $\frac{1}{2}$ pint (1$\frac{1}{4}$ cups) milk
salt   3 oz. ($\frac{3}{4}$ cup)
1 oz. (2T) butter   grated cheese
2 tablespoons (2$\frac{1}{2}$T) flour   pepper

Trim the roots and green part from the leeks. Wash very
thoroughly, then cook in boiling salted water for 10 minutes
or until just tender. Drain and arrange in a shallow 2 pint
(5 cup) ovenproof dish, reserving 4 tablespoons (5T) cooking
liquor.
Make a roux with the butter and flour, blend in the milk and
reserved cooking liquor and bring to boiling point, stirring.
Add most of the cheese and season well. Pour the sauce over
the leeks and sprinkle with the remaining cheese. Cook under
a medium grill (broiler) for about 5 minutes.
Serves 4

Braised Chicory

Endives braisés
In France chicory is endive and endive is chicory – all very muddling.
Chicory is often thought to be rather bitter when cooked. I find it best to
braise it, adding a little sugar.

1½ lb. chicory
1 oz. (2T) butter
3 tablespoons (3¾T) water
1 teaspoon lemon juice
1 teaspoon castor (superfine)
    sugar

½ teaspoon salt
⅛ teaspoon freshly ground
    black pepper

Put the chicory in a pan of boiling water and boil for 2
minutes. Drain in a colander and rinse with cold water.
Butter a 2 pint (5 cup) shallow ovenproof dish with half of the
butter. Arrange the chicory in the dish. Add the remaining
ingredients and dot with the remaining butter. Cover with a
piece of greaseproof paper, then a lid. Cook at 300°F, Gas Mark
2 for 1-1¼ hours until tender.
Lift carefully from the pan and serve with the juices from the
dish.
Serves 4

Chicory with Cheese

Endives au gratin

1½ oz. (3T) butter
8 small heads of chicory,
    quartered lengthways
juice of 1 lemon
1 teaspoon castor (superfine)
    sugar
¼ teaspoon salt

pinch of pepper

Cheese topping:
2 oz. (½ cup) Cheddar cheese,
    grated
1 oz. (¼ cup) Parmesan cheese,
    grated

Use $\frac{1}{2}$ oz. (1T) butter to grease a shallow $1\frac{1}{2}$ pint (4 cup) ovenproof casserole. Add chicory and lemon juice and turn well to coat with lemon. Dot with the remaining butter and add sugar and seasoning. Cover tightly and cook at 350°F, Gas Mark 4 for about 45 minutes or until tender. Baste once or twice while cooking.

Clean the sides of the dish with a hot moist cloth. Sprinkle with cheese and return to the oven to brown for a further 30 minutes.

Serves 4

Hollandaise Sauce

Sauce hollandaise

2 tablespoons ($2\frac{1}{2}$T) wine
    vinegar
2 tablespoons ($2\frac{1}{2}$T) lemon
    juice
2 bay leaves
2 blades mace

6 peppercorns
3 egg yolks
4 oz. ($\frac{1}{2}$ cup) butter
salt
pepper

Put the vinegar, lemon juice, bay leaves, mace and pepper-corns into a small pan and simmer until the liquor has reduced to 2 tablespoons ($2\frac{1}{2}$T). Put the egg yolks into a small bowl, blend in the strained liquor from the pan and mix well.

Put the bowl on top of a pan of hot, *not* boiling water. Beat in a knob of soft butter and then whisk the mixture over the heat until it has thickened. Gradually add the remaining butter. Whisk constantly and remove the bowl from the heat if the sauce thickens too quickly. When finished the sauce should form very soft peaks. Add salt and pepper to taste. Keep the sauce warm by standing it in a bowl over warm, not hot, water until required.

Serves 4

Aïoli Sauce

Sauce Aïoli

2 or 3 garlic cloves, crushed
3 egg yolks
$\frac{1}{3}$ pint (scant 1 cup)
   vegetable or nut oil

$\frac{1}{2}$ teaspoon salt
$\frac{1}{2}$ teaspoon pepper
2 tablespoons ($2\frac{1}{2}$T)
   lemon juice

Blend the garlic and egg yolks in a bowl. Gradually whisk in the oil as for mayonnaise. Stir in the seasoning and lemon juice. Serve as a dip with fresh pieces of raw vegetables.

Vegetables Aïoli

Aïoli

Aïoli, see above
$\frac{1}{2}$ small white cabbage,
   finely shredded

4 oz. salami, cut in pieces
2 oz. black olives
4 hard-boiled eggs, quartered

Make the aïoli as above.
Arrange the cabbage on a serving dish. Top with the salami, olives and egg quarters. Pour over the aïoli sauce just before serving.
Serves 4

Artichokes

Artichauts
Serve globe artichokes hot with hollandaise sauce, see page 65, or a carton of soured cream blended with three tablespoons ($3\frac{3}{4}$T) of well seasoned French dressing, see page 70.

4 globe artichokes   salt

Cut off the leaf points with scissors. Boil a large pan of salted water, add the artichokes. Cover and simmer for about 20 minutes, until tender. (A leaf will pull off easily when the artichokes are cooked.) Drain thoroughly before serving.
Serves 4

Chicory and Endive Salad

Salade d'endives et de chicorie

2 small heads of chicory
1 small endive, shredded
1 dessert apple,
   peeled and cored
juice of $\frac{1}{2}$ lemon
4 sticks celery, chopped

1 oz. (3T) walnuts, chopped
$\frac{1}{2}$ small onion, chopped
8 tablespoons (10T)
   French dressing, see page 86
salt
pepper

Cut the chicory in $\frac{1}{2}$ inch slices. Soak in iced water with the endive for 10 minutes. Mix the apple with the lemon juice in a bowl.
Drain the chicory and endive, add to the apple with the other ingredients. Check seasoning before serving.
Serves 4

Ratatouille

2 small aubergines (eggplant)
4 courgettes (zucchini)
salt
6 tablespoons ($7\frac{1}{2}$T) olive oil
2 medium onions, finely sliced
2 green peppers, de-seeded
   and thinly sliced

1 garlic clove, crushed
1 lb. tomatoes, skinned,
   de-seeded and chopped
pepper
1 tablespoon ($1\frac{1}{4}$T) chopped
   parsley

Cut the unpeeled aubergines (egg plant) and courgettes (zucchini) in $\frac{1}{2}$ inch cubes. Place on a piece of kitchen paper and sprinkle with salt. Leave to drain for 30 minutes.

Heat the olive oil in a large heavy pan. Add the onions and cook slowly until soft but not coloured.

Dry the aubergines (egg plant) and courgettes (zucchini) with kitchen paper then add them to the pan with the green peppers and garlic. Cover and simmer very gently for about 40 minutes. Stir occasionally so the mixture does not stick. Add the tomatoes and pepper to taste. Cover and cook for a further 20 minutes.

Stir in the parsley and serve hot as an accompanying vegetable or cold as an hors d'oeuvre.

Serves 4-6

Potato and Celery Salad

Salade de pommes de terre et céleri

1 lb. potatoes
salt
6 tablespoons (7½T) French
   dressing
1 small head of celery,
   chopped
2 large, sweet gherkins, sliced

¼ pint (½ cup + 2T)
   mayonnaise, see page 87
salt
pepper
1 tablespoon (1¼T) chopped
   chives

Boil the potatoes in salted water in the usual way then drain, toss in French dressing and leave until cold.
Slice the potatoes into a bowl, add the celery, gherkins and mayonnaise and season well. Add most of the chives then cover and leave in a cool place until required. Sprinkle with the remaining chives before serving.
Serves 4-6

French Dressing

Sauce vinaigrette

½ garlic clove, crushed
½ teaspoon dry mustard
¼ teaspoon salt
½ teaspoon freshly ground
   black pepper
1 teaspoon very finely
   chopped onion or a few
   finely chopped chives

1 teaspoon castor (superfine)
   sugar
¼ pint (½ cup + 2T) olive,
   vegetable or corn oil
4-6 tablespoons (5-7½T) white
   wine vinegar or cider
   vinegar (or half each
   vinegar and lemon juice)

Blend the first six ingredients together in a bowl. Mix in the oil slowly with a whisk or spoon. Finally stir in the vinegar or vinegar and lemon juice. Taste and adjust the seasoning if necessary.

For a simpler French dressing that will keep, omit the chives or onion and lemon juice. Put all the ingredients together in a screw-top jar, replace the lid and shake vigorously until well blended. In this way, the ingredients can be proportionately increased and more made at one time. The dressing can be kept in the jar in a cool place for up to six weeks.

Mayonnaise

2 egg yolks
$\frac{1}{2}$ teaspoon made mustard
$\frac{1}{2}$ teaspoon salt
$\frac{1}{8}$ teaspoon freshly ground
  black pepper
$\frac{1}{2}$ teaspoon castor (superfine)
  sugar

$\frac{1}{2}$ pint ($1\frac{1}{4}$ cups) olive,
  vegetable or corn oil
1 tablespoon ($1\frac{1}{4}$T) lemon
  juice
1 tablespoon ($1\frac{1}{4}$T) white
  wine vinegar or cider
  vinegar

Stand a bowl on a damp cloth to prevent it from slipping on the table. Put in the egg yolks, mustard, salt, pepper and sugar. Mix thoroughly, then add the oil drop by drop, beating well with a whisk the whole time, until the sauce is thick and smooth. Beat in the vinegar and lemon juice. This makes a thick, traditional mayonnaise. Add a little thin cream or top of the milk for a thinner mixture.

Should the sauce curdle through adding the oil too quickly to the egg yolks, take a fresh egg yolk and begin again, adding the curdled mayonnaise very slowly in the same way as the oil is added to the original egg yolks.

INTERMISSION: CAKES AND PASTRIES

No book on French cooking would be complete without a section on cakes and pastries, those mouth-watering delicacies which adorn the windows of *patisseries* throughout the country.

Little Nun Cakes

Les petites religieuses

Choux pastry
$\frac{1}{4}$ pint ($\frac{1}{2}$ cup + 2T) milk
    and water, mixed
$1\frac{1}{2}$ oz. (3T) butter
pinch of salt
$2\frac{1}{2}$ oz. ($\frac{1}{2}$ cup + 2T) plain
    (all-purpose) flour
2 eggs
Pastry cream:
2 eggs
2 oz. ($\frac{1}{4}$ cup) castor
    (superfine) sugar
1 oz. (2T) plain
    (all-purpose) flour
$\frac{1}{2}$ pint ($1\frac{1}{4}$ cups) milk
few drops vanilla essence

Chocolate glacé icing:
2 oz. (2 squares) plain
    chocolate
nob of butter
6 oz. (1 cup + 2T) icing
    (confectioners') sugar, sifted
water

Chocolate butter icing:
$1\frac{1}{2}$ oz. (3T) butter
3 oz. ($\frac{1}{2}$ cup) icing
    (confectioners') sugar, sifted
1 oz. (1 square) plain
    chocolate, melted

Put the milk and water, butter and salt into a pan. Heat gently until the butter has melted then bring to the boil. Remove from the heat, add the flour and stir until smooth. Cook for 1 minute, stirring. Cool the mixture slightly, then gradually beat in the eggs. Beat until the mixture leaves the sides of the pan. Put the paste into a large piping bag fitted with a $\frac{1}{2}$ inch plain pipe. Dampen some baking trays. Pipe 9 balls of $1\frac{1}{2}$ inch diameter and 9 balls of $\frac{1}{2}$ inch diameter. Bake at 400°F, Gas Mark 6 for 25-30 minutes until crisp and golden. Make a slit in each bun so the steam can escape. Cool on a wire rack. Whisk the egg yolks with the sugar for the pastry cream until pale. Blend in the flour and a little of the milk. Boil the rest of the milk then pour on to the egg mixture, stirring well. Return to the pan and cook for 2-3 minutes, stirring. Cool slightly. Whisk the egg whites until stiff then fold into the pastry cream with the vanilla essence. When cold, use to fill the choux buns. Melt the chocolate with the butter for the glacé icing in a bowl placed over a pan of hot water. When melted, stir in the icing (confectioners') sugar. Add just enough water to make a thick glacé icing. Use to coat the top of the large buns. Place a small bun on top of each and coat with icing. Leave to set.

Beat together all the ingredients for the butter icing. Leave in a cold place until stiff enough to pipe. Using a small rose pipe and a forcing bag, pipe rosettes of chocolate butter-cream round the bases of each small bun to give a wreath effect.
Makes 9

Florentines

2 oz. ($\frac{1}{4}$ cup) butter
2 oz. ($\frac{1}{4}$ cup) castor
(superfine) sugar
2 oz. ($\frac{1}{3}$ cup) mixed walnuts
and almonds, chopped finely
$\frac{1}{2}$ oz. (1T) candied peel,
chopped

$\frac{1}{2}$ oz. (1T) glacé cherries,
chopped
$\frac{1}{2}$ oz. (1T) sultanas, chopped
1 tablespoon (1$\frac{1}{4}$T) thin
(coffee) cream
3 oz. (3 squares) plain
chocolate, melted

Melt the butter in a pan, then add the sugar. Boil for 1 minute. Add nuts, peel, cherries and sultanas to pan with the cream. Grease 2 or 3 baking trays well. Put teaspoons of the mixture on the baking trays, allowing plenty of room for them to spread. Bake at 350°F, Gas Mark 4 for 10 minutes or until deep golden brown. Remove from the oven and press into shape with a palette knife. Allow to cool slightly before lifting on to a wire rack to cool.

Spread melted chocolate over the backs of the florentines with a palette knife. Make wavy patterns with a fork. Leave to set.
Makes about 20

Brioches

3 tablespoons ($3\frac{3}{4}$T) water
$\frac{1}{2}$ oz. (2 teaspoons) dried yeast
$\frac{1}{2}$ teaspoon castor (superfine) sugar
8 oz. (2 cups) plain (all-purpose) flour
$\frac{1}{2}$ teaspoon salt
$\frac{1}{2}$ oz. (1T) castor (superfine) sugar

2 eggs, beaten
2 oz. ($\frac{1}{4}$ cup) butter, melted and cooled

Egg glaze:
1 egg
1 tablespoon ($1\frac{1}{4}$T) cold water,
pinch of sugar, all blended together

Grease twelve 3-inch brioche tins well, or use deep fluted patty (muffin) tins. Heat the water until lukewarm and pour into a small bowl. Whisk in the yeast and $\frac{1}{2}$ teaspoon castor (superfine) sugar. Leave in a warm place for about 10 minutes, until the yeast has dissolved and froth appears.

Sift the flour and salt into a bowl. Mix in the remaining sugar. Stir in the yeast mixture, eggs and butter. Beat by hand until the mixture leaves the sides of the bowl. Knead on a lightly floured board for 5 minutes. Place the dough in a slightly oiled polythene bag and leave to rise at room temperature until it has doubled in size and springs back when lightly pressed with a finger – this takes about $1\frac{1}{2}$ hours.

Knead well on a lightly floured board for about 5 minutes. Divide the dough in 4 equal pieces, then each piece in 3. With each piece, use about $\frac{3}{4}$ to form a ball. Place the balls of dough in tins and firmly press a hole in the centre. Place the remaining small piece of dough in the hole.

Place the tins on a baking tray. Cover with a large, oiled polythene bag. Leave to rise in a warm place until light and puffy, about 1 hour. Brush lightly with egg glaze. Bake at 450°F, Gas Mark 8 for about 10 minutes. Serve warm.
Makes 12

Dark Chocolate Cake

Gâteau au chocolat

2½ oz. (½ cup + 2T) self-
  raising (all-purpose) flour
½ oz. (2T) cocoa
4 oz. (4 squares) plain
  chocolate
4 oz. (½ cup) butter
4 oz. (½ cup) castor
  (superfine) sugar
4 eggs, separated

Filling:
4 rounded tablespoons (5T)
  apricot jam

1 tablespoon (1¼T) water

Icing:
6 oz. (good cup) icing
  (confectioners') sugar,
  sieved
½ oz. (2T) cocoa
2 oz. (¼ cup) butter
2 oz. (2 squares) plain
  chocolate
2 tablespoons (2½T) milk

Line an 8 inch cake tin with greased greaseproof paper. Sift
together the flour and cocoa. Melt the chocolate in a small
bowl over a pan of simmering water, remove from the heat
then cool.
Beat the butter and sugar until pale and creamy. Beat in the
egg yolks one at a time, beating well after each addition. Fold
in the flour mixture alternately with the melted chocolate.
Whisk the egg whites until they form soft peaks, fold into the
cake mixture. Turn into the prepared tin, bake at 350°F, Gas
Mark 4 for about 50 minutes or until a skewer inserted in the
centre comes out clean. Turn the cake out on a wire rack to
cool. Cut in three layers when cold.
Put the filling ingredients in a pan, bring to the boil and
simmer for 1 minute, then sieve. Brush the cut surfaces of the
cake with half the filling. Reassemble on the wire rack. Brush
the top and sides of the cake with remaining filling.
Sift together the icing sugar and cocoa for the icing. Heat
the remaining ingredients together gently in a pan until the
butter and chocolate have melted. Remove from the heat, add
the sifted ingredients and beat until thick. Spread the icing
quickly over the cake and leave in a cool place to become firm.

Magali

2 oz. ($\frac{1}{4}$ cup) butter
2 oz. ($\frac{1}{4}$ cup) castor
 (superfine) sugar
few drops of vanilla essence
4 oz. (1 cup) plain
 (all-purpose) flour
3 oz. (3 squares) plain
 chocolate

1 egg yolk
$\frac{1}{2}$ oz. (1T) unsalted butter
4 tablespoons (5T) thick
 (heavy) cream
2 teaspoons rum or fruit
 squash
6 oz. (1 cup + 2T) icing
 (confectioners') sugar

Grease about 18 individual, fairly shallow patty (muffin) tins.
Cream the butter and sugar together until lighter in colour,
add the vanilla essence and egg yolk. Work the flour into the
mixture. Roll out the pastry thinly on a floured board and use
to line the patty tins. Prick the bases with a fork, then bake at
375°F, Gas Mark 5 for 10-15 minutes until golden brown.
Remove from the tins and cool on a wire rack.
Melt the chocolate, butter and cream in a pan over gentle heat,
stirring continuously. Remove from the heat, add rum and
allow to cool completely, beating occasionally until thick.
Divide between the pastry cases. Add enough water to the
icing (confectioners') sugar to make a thick glacé icing. Spoon
over the chocolate mixture and decorate with a chocolate curl
or piece of flaked chocolate bar. Leave to set.
Makes 18

MAGALI (*Photograph: Cadbury Schweppes Food Advisory Service, Bournville Birmingham, England*)

Basque Cake

Gâteau Basque
Serve Gâteau Basque for dessert or at tea time

Pastry cream:
2 egg yolks
2 oz. ($\frac{1}{4}$ cup) castor
  (superfine) sugar
$\frac{1}{2}$ pint (1$\frac{1}{4}$ cups) milk

2 tablespoons (2$\frac{1}{2}$T)
  cornflour (cornstarch)
1 egg white
few drops of vanilla essence

Beat together the egg yolks, one teaspoon of the sugar, the cornflour (cornstarch) and sufficient milk to make a smooth paste. Boil the remaining milk, pour on to the egg mixture and return to the pan. Simmer until thickened then remove from the heat.

Whisk the egg white until stiff then whisk in the remaining sugar and vanilla essence. Fold in to the boiled mixture and leave until cold.

Pastry:
12 oz. (3 cups) self-raising
  (all-purpose) flour
2 oz. ($\frac{1}{2}$ cup) cornflour
  (cornstarch)
6 oz. ($\frac{3}{4}$ cup) butter
8 oz. (1 cup) castor (superfine)
  sugar

2 eggs
1 egg yolk
grated rind of 1 lemon
about 1 tablespoon (1$\frac{1}{4}$T)
  lemon juice or brandy

Sift together the flour and cornflour (cornstarch). Cream the butter and sugar until soft then add the eggs and yolk, together with the lemon rind. Work in the flour and enough lemon juice or brandy to give a soft rolling consistency. Cover and chill for 30 minutes.

Use half the pastry to line the base and sides of an 11 inch loose-bottomed fluted flan tin. Press the pastry into place with the fingers as it is very soft. Spread the pastry cream on top. Cover with the remaining pastry. Bake at 350°F, Gas Mark 4 for about 45 minutes or until the pastry is golden brown.
Serves about 10

LAST ACT: DESSERTS

Most French families finish their meals with fresh fruit and cheese, but even when special desserts are served the dish is usually fairly light. French schoolchildren visiting Britain go overboard for rolypoly and suet pudding but this is because they have no equivalent at home. In this chapter, I have concentrated on delicate, rich dishes which the French do so well.

Fruit and Cheese Dessert

Le fromage et les fruits

Serve a selection of French cheeses such as Camembert and Brie with iced melon balls, black grapes, radishes, stuffed olives and pears. They look beautiful arranged on vine leaves with a bunch of green grapes. If no vine leaves are available use blackcurrant leaves.

Floating Islands

Iles flottantes

1½ pints (3¾ cups) milk
few drops of vanilla essence
3 eggs, separated

5 oz. (½ cup + 2T) castor
  (superfine) sugar
few fresh strawberries

Heat the milk to simmering point in a large pan. Add the
vanilla essence. Whisk 2 egg whites until stiff then whisk in
4 oz. (½ cup) of sugar a teaspoon at a time, whisking well after
each addition.
Place tablespoons of meringue on top of the milk and poach
for 10 minutes, until set. Place meringue 'islands' on a plate.
Strain the milk and measure 1 pint (2½ cups). Beat together
the egg yolks, remaining egg and remaining sugar. Pour on
the measured milk, return to the pan and heat gently, without
simmering, until thickened.
Strain the custard into a large shallow dish. Lay the 'islands'
on top and serve with fresh strawberries. Serve warm or cold.
Serves 4

Blackcurrant Sorbet

Sorbet au cassis

15 oz. can blackcurrants
6 oz. ($\frac{3}{4}$ cup) granulated
   sugar
grated rind and juice of
   1 lemon

1 teaspoon powdered gelatine
1 tablespoon ($1\frac{1}{4}$T) water
2 egg whites

Drain the blackcurrants, reserving the juice. Make the juice up to $\frac{3}{4}$ pint (2 cups) with water and put it in a pan with the sugar. Heat gently until the sugar has dissolved, stirring occasionally. Simmer for 2 minutes, remove from the heat and add the lemon rind and juice.

Dissolve the gelatine with the water in a bowl over a pan of simmering water. Sieve the blackcurrants then stir the purée into the sugar syrup with the gelatine. Turn the mixture into a plastic container, cover it and leave in the freezing compartment of the refrigerator, or in the deep-freeze until almost frozen.

Put the mixture in a bowl and whisk until smooth. Whisk the egg whites until they form soft peaks, fold into the blackcurrant mixture. Return to the plastic container, cover and freeze until required. Serve with Cigarette Biscuits (see page 108).

Serves 6

Fruit Fritters

Beignets de fruits

7 oz. (1¾ cups) plain (all-purpose) flour
1 oz. (2T) castor (superfine) sugar
⅜ pint (1 cup) white wine
1 tablespoon (1¼T) olive oil
grated rind of ½ lemon
3 eggs, separated
3 dessert apples, peeled, cored and finely chopped

1 oz. (2T) dried apricots, finely chopped
1 oz. (2T) sultanas
1½ oz. (¼ cup) blanched almonds, finely chopped
1 tablespoon (1¼T) rum
oil for deep frying
extra castor (superfine) sugar

Put the flour and sugar in a bowl. Make a well in the centre and pour in the wine, olive oil and lemon rind. Mix well then beat in the egg yolks. Leave the batter in a cool place until required.

Put the apples, apricots, sultanas and almonds in a bowl with the rum and leave to macerate for 1 hour.

Whisk the egg whites until they form stiff peaks then fold them into the batter with the fruit mixture. Put tablespoons of the mixture into very hot fat and fry for a few seconds until golden brown. Drain on kitchen paper. Sprinkle liberally with castor (superfine) sugar and serve at once.

Serves 4-6

Profiteroles

Choux pastry:
2 oz. ($\frac{1}{4}$ cup) butter
$\frac{1}{4}$ pint ($\frac{1}{2}$ cup + 2T) milk and
  water, mixed
$2\frac{1}{2}$ oz. (good $\frac{1}{2}$ cup) plain
  (all-purpose) flour, sifted
2 eggs, beaten

Filling and icing:
$\frac{1}{2}$ pint ($1\frac{1}{4}$ cups) thick (heavy)
  cream, lightly whipped
8 oz. ($1\frac{1}{2}$ cups) icing
  (confectioners') sugar
1 tablespoon ($1\frac{1}{4}$T) cocoa
1 tablespoon ($1\frac{1}{4}$T) rum
1-2 tablespoons ($1\frac{1}{4}$-$2\frac{1}{2}$T)
  warm water

Put the butter, milk and water in a small pan and bring to the boil. Remove the pan from the heat, add the flour all at once and beat the mixture until it forms a ball. Gradually beat in the eggs to make a smooth, shiny paste.

Put the mixture in a large piping bag fitted with a $\frac{1}{2}$ inch plain nozzle. Pipe 20 blobs on to a greased baking tray. Bake at 425°F, Gas Mark 7 for 10 minutes, then reduce the oven temperature to 375°F, Gas Mark 5 for a further 15 to 20 minutes until golden brown. Split one side of each bun so the steam can escape. Cool on a wire rack.

Fill each bun with whipped cream. Sift the icing sugar and cocoa into a bowl. Stir in the rum and sufficient warm water to make a thick glacé icing. Spear each bun with a fork and dip the tops in icing. Pile up in a pyramid as each one is finished. Serve the same day.

Serves 6

PROFITEROLES *(Photograph: Cadbury Schweppes Food Advisory Service,*
  Bournville, Birmingham, England)

Scorched Oranges

Oranges brûlées
Serve very cold.

4 large oranges
2 tablespoons (2½T) Grand
  Marnier or Orange Curacao
two 5 oz. cartons (1¼ cups)
  soured cream

½ pint (1¼ cups) thick (heavy)
  cream, lightly whipped
2 oz. (¼ cup) Demerara (raw)
  sugar

Peel the oranges, removing all pith, and slice thinly. Place in
a shallow 2 pint (5 cup) ovenproof dish, sprinkle with the
liqueur. Blend together the soured cream and thick (heavy)
cream and spread over the oranges. Chill thoroughly in the
refrigerator.
Sprinkle the sugar on top Heat the grill (broiler) to maximum,
place the dish underneath. When the sugar has just melted
remove the dish from the heat.
Serves 4-6

Crêpes Suzette

*For entertaining, prepare both the pancakes and the sauce in advance and
assemble just before serving, heating the pancakes in the sauce.*

Batter:
4 oz. (1 cup) plain
  (all-purpose) flour
¼ teaspoon salt
2 eggs
scant ½ pint (1 cup) milk
1 tablespoon (1¼T) melted
  butter, or oil
1 tablespoon (1¼T) oil for
  frying

Sauce:
4 oz. (½ cup) castor
  (superfine) sugar
4 oz. (½ cup) butter
juice of 2 oranges
finely grated rind of 1 orange
1 tablespoon (1¼T) of either
  Curacao, Grand Marnier or
  other orange liqueur
3 tablespoons (3¾T) brandy

Sift the flour and salt into a large bowl. Add the egg, then gradually beat in the milk to make a smooth batter. Stir in the butter or oil.

Put the oil for frying in a 6 or 7 inch heavy based frying pan and heat slowly. When it is really hot pour off the excess oil and spoon about 2 tablespoons ($2\frac{1}{2}$T) of the batter into the pan. Tip the pan slightly from side to side so that the batter thinly covers the base of the pan. Cook the pancake for about 1 minute, then turn it over and cook for another minute. Put the pancake on a plate and cover with a clean tea towel.

Repeat with the remaining batter, stacking the pancakes on top of each other.

Put the sugar, butter, orange rind and juice into a pan. Heat gently until the sugar has dissolved, then simmer the sauce for about 5 to 10 minutes until syrupy.

Put a pancake in the pan, fold it in four, remove from the pan, place on a hot serving dish and keep it hot. Repeat with the remaining pancakes.

When they have all been coated add the liqueur and brandy to the pan, and replace the folded pancakes. Reheat the sauce gently then serve the pancakes.

Note   To flambé:
Add liqueur only to the pan before replacing the pancakes. Reheat gently. Warm the brandy, pour over the pancakes and set alight.
Serves 4

Index

(Figures in italics refer to illustrations)

A
Aioli sauce 66
Almonds, trout with 53
Artichokes 68
Artichokes, French dressed
    globe 25
Asparagus 62, *63*
Aubergines, baked eggs with 28

B
Bacon and onion quiche 54, *55*
Baked eggs with aubergines 28
Baked onions, French 58
Bayonne lamb 41, *42*
Basque cake *79*, 80
Beef
    burgundy 36
    fillet in pastry 33
    pepperpot 37, *38*
Blackcurrant sorbet 84
Bouillabaisse 13, *14*
Braised chicory 64
Brandade of kipper 17
Brioches 74, *75*
Burgundy beef 44

C
Cakes
    basque *79*, 80
    dark chocolate 76
    little nun 73
Casserole, veal 51
Cauliflower soup 10, *11*
Celery salad, potato and 70
Cheese, chicory with 64
Cheese, fruit and, dessert 81
Cheese, leeks with 62
Cheese soufflé *23*, 24
Chicken
    in wine 48
    tarragon 49
Chicory and endive salad 68
Chicory with cheese 64
Chicory, braised 64
Chocolate cake, dark 76
Cod, saute of 52
Consommé, eggs in 20
Country fried potatoes 61
Courgette (zucchini) fritters 60
Cream sauce, pork in 40
Crêpes suzette 89, *91*
Crudités 24
Cucumber sauce, sole with 56
Curry sauce, eggs in 28

D
Dark chocolate cake 76
Dauphine potatoes 61
Dressing, French 70
Duchess potatoes 58
Duck with orange 50, *51*

E
Eggs
    baked with aubergines 28
    in consommé 20
    in curry sauce 28

mornay 21
Endive salad, chicory and 68

F
Floating islands 82, *83*
Florentines 72
Fritters
    courgette (zucchini) 60
    fruit 85, *86*
French baked onions 58
French dressed globe
    artichokes 25
French dressing 70
French omelette 57
French onion soup *15*, 16
Fresh herb pâté 17
Fresh salmon with prawns 52
Fruit and cheese dessert 81
Fruit fritters 85, *86*

G
Garlic bread 10
Globe artichokes, French
    dressed 25

H
Hollandaise sauce 65

I
Individual quiches *31*, 32

K
Kipper, brandade of 17

L
Lamb
    bayonne 41, *42*
    in pastry *43*, 44
Leeks with cheese 62
Little nun cakes 73
Lyonnaise potatoes *59*, 60

M
Mackerel, smoked, pâté 16
Magali 77, *78*
Mayonnaise 71
Mushroom cream soup 12
Mushroom vols au vent 29, *30*
Mussels marinière, 18, *19*

O
Omelette, French 57
Onion, bacon and, quiche 54, *55*
Onions, French baked 58
Onion soup, French *15*, 16
Orange
    duck with 50, *51*
    scorched 89

P
Pastry
    beef fillet in 33
    lamb in *43*, 44
    shortcrust 32
Pâté
    fresh herb 17
    maison 20, *22*

smoked mackerel 16
Pepperpot beef 37, *38*
Peppers, stuffed 9
Pissaladière 26, *27*
Pork
    fillet in wine 39
    in cream sauce 40
Pot roast 34, *35*
Potato and celery salad 70
Potatoes
    country fried 61
    dauphine 61
    duchess 58
    lyonnaise *59*, 60
Prawns, fresh salmon with 52
Profiteroles *87*, 88

Q
Quiches
    bacon and onion 54, *55*
    individual *31*, 32

R
Ratatouille 69

S
Salad
    chicory and endive 68
    potato and celery 70
Salmon, fresh, with prawns 52
Sauce
    aioli 66
    hollandaise 65
Sauté of cod 52
Scorched oranges 89
Shortcrust pastry 32
Smoked mackerel pâté 16
Sole with cucumber sauce 56
Sorbet
    blackcurrant 84
Soufflé, cheese *23*, 24
Soup
    bouillabaise 13, *14*
    cauliflower 10, *11*
    French onion *15*, 16
    mushroom cream 12
    tomato herb 16
Stuffed peppers 9

T
Tarragon chicken 49
Tomato herb soup 12
Trout with almonds 53

V
Veal birds 46, *47*
Veal casserole 45
Vegetable aioli 66, *67*
Vols au vent, mushroom 29, *30*

W
Wine
    chicken in 48

Z
Zucchini see courgette

PDO 82-0016